Ring Along the River

Ring Along the River

Poems by

Robert Nordstrom

Cover design by Shay Culligan
Cover image by Eric Nordstrom
Lotus figure by Anh Le on Unsplash
Author photo by Robert Nordstrom

ISBN: 979-8-90146-834-0

Kelsay Books
502 South 1040 East, A-119
American Fork, Utah 84003
Kelsaybooks.com

For Linda—best friend and life partner—
who, with love, humility and example,
has kept me open and looking outward
for nearly a half century now.

Acknowledgments

Thank you to the following publications, where versions of the following poems previously appeared:

ONE ART: A Journal of Poetry: "Dear Mother," "The Naked Truth"

Third Wednesday: "On the Other Side of the Door"

Verse-Virtual: "Abeyance," "Arrogance," "Choice," "Conspiracy Theories," "Conundrum," "Fortune and Misfortune," "God Joke," "Loss," "Mashed Potatoes Love," "Mother's Spaces," "Packing for Vacation," "Pitching In," "Secrets," "Terror," "Who's Who," "Zero Sum Conjunction"

Contents

II. Big Thoughts

Sing Along

Ring along the river
the takers and the givers
little thoughts big thoughts
we all fall in

I.
Little Thoughts

Lying in Bed Late at Night

the window rattles:
am I trying to get in
or invited out?

Sleep

daylit puzzle
overturned

pieces scattered
and speeding

away

Like Magic

flapped sheet floats
like a magician's silk
over a bed full of dreams
new human arises
when morning arrives

Searching

what occurs
bends the knee
to the reason for
and meaning of
what occurs

Who's Who

I am confounded
standing before the mirror
him and me again?

Talking Politics with Dr. Seuss

I think you think I think that
when actually I think this
and think you think that
which come to think of it
thinking this ’n that
is not a bad way to think
when thinking

Conundrum

back then I was there
now I ask how I got here
when here's now there then

Unexpected Gift

Tables and chairs filled
I'm asked to sit over there
then see what they can't

Sisyphus

pulls away
to push forward
and not fall back

Soft Landing

the angel appears
when saturated with life
the heart opens wide

Loss

For Anne

what was is no more
an intimacy unwound
my love hold me close

Sympathy Card Conundrum

I search for words to express
what I feel you must be feeling
if I was feeling what you must be feeling

Packing for Vacation

Young friends say have fun.
Older friends say please be safe.
Band-aids or beach balls?

Terror

Rebel brow breaks free.
Wife approaches scissors in hand.
Surrender or run?

Airline Attendant Ayn Rand Presents Flight Safety Instructions

If problems occur
the oxygen masks will drop:
forget the children.

Short Story

A new puppy
likely our last

Turning Pages

is what we do
like it or not
withstanding

Clicks & Ticks

Older now I find
I take more photos of you
as if to stop time

Questions Versus Answers

Science is humble
religion is hubristic
even God knows this

Arrogance

Billions and billions
of earth-like planets, they say,
but God looks like us.

God Joke

Abe obeyed God's charge:
Issac's up there, here's the knife—
never mind, kidding.

End Times Prophesies

The prophetic precludes
the possible, the outlandish
replaces the plausible.
Our jealous God, so much like us,
the mirror before which we bow.

Pitching In

I asked God
but he was busy
so I forgave myself

Conspiracy Theories

I open my eyes
So many things to believe
I close them again

The TV and Credenza

Our grandchildren smile
into their future. Above
disturbing news lurks.

Grandchildren

I am the past
they are asked to remember
they are the future
I am tasked to imagine

Waiting for the Dog to Do Her Business

Hole in the night sky,
blue eye of God peeking through.
I stand here alone.

I Believe

nowhere is somewhere
today will be yesterday
a matter of faith

II.
Big Thoughts

What Is It?

Just tell it, as they say,
like it is,

but if you don't know what it is,
merely announce,

it is what it is.
Who can argue with a five-word five-syllable tautology

designed to end a conversation,
scuttle an investigation, punctuate a presentation

parading as proclamation,
while offering

a prognostication
explaining what is

must always be it,
though truth be told,

with the lights turned up
and the beer mug empty,

you have merely surrendered,
given up, tossed in the towel,

thrown chaff to the wind, and remain clueless
as to what it is you are even talking about?

Listening to the News

I've heard enough
and I'll never vote again.

I've heard enough
and I'll cast my ballot in the morning.

I've heard enough
to believe prayer is the only answer.

I've heard enough
to know God is likely napping.

I've heard enough, I've heard enough
to fall in love

with the way she thumb-tucks
a rebellious strand of hair

behind her ear
without mangling

a single distressing syllable,
then smiles at the camera

fetchingly. But I digress,
tilt off track,

which tends to happen
when beleaguered by news,

primarily bad,
and beauty,

no matter how superficial,
becomes my stumbling way forward.

It’s Only Tuesday

eleven murdered in a synagogue
child dropped dead in a school hallway
life stock tanked in a pool of blood
before markets correct
then slowly rise

Zero-Sum Conjunction

My son and I talk politics
agree about everything
but it still feels like argument.

I wish to say *but* . . .
but fear *but*
has become a zero-sum

conjunction this evening
so I stare instead
at the ceiling

fan barely stirring
the humid air
in a family's room

where we agree
finally
on silence.

Keeping the Peace

the thing I wish
to say but
must not

hovers
like crow
soiling pale blue sky

indigo period
ellipsis of silence
hanging in the room's thin air

she
who needs to know
but does not wish to hear

me
who wishes to say
but must not

Family Dinner Table

As children
at the dropleaf dinner table
next to the window
overlooking the driveway,
I sat on the right
because my brother ate with his left.
Later, as adults,
we switched sides,
me on the left, he on the right,
our elbows sometimes sharp
as we ingested and digested
the day's news
trying to keep
our mouths shut.

The Naked Truth

I stand naked inside the closet
where my costumes hang,

each more authentic than the others
when buttoned and zipped

into today. But here, before the mirror,
the naked body sags into tomorrow,

offering pause and gratitude
dressed in breath

before the light switch clicks
and the door blows shut.

Fortune & Misfortune

The foot of my seven-year-old granddaughter's
new toy dragon breaks off and she's devastated.

On the way home, her five-year-old sister
cuddles her toy dragon lovingly and says,
"I'm glad my dragon didn't lose its foot."

Years ago, Pat Robertson said Hurricane Katrina
was God's punishment for New Orleans sins
while basking beneath blue skies in his backyard.

At the corner a homeless man curled in the grass
slaps at a fly. I sip my coffee, still hot, and drive on.

Abeyance

my granddaughter's foot
so sculpturally perfect

toes raised
instep like an arched brow

eager to run
fearlessly

across concrete and dirt
pebbles and stones

tender and vulnerable
flesh held loosely

in abeyance

each step and stride
her indelible imprint

on the hard earth
below

Contests

They collapse on the ball
like a hive of bees
around a pot of honey.
Feet, legs, elbows flailing
the ball pops out of the scrum
onto my granddaughter's foot
and into the net,
her first goal ever.

After the game
I pull out a piece of hard candy,
hold out two fists
and tell her to choose.
Good fortune still on her side
she chooses correctly.
I pull out another piece,
state the rule—*no chewing allowed.*
On the count of three
we pop them into our mouths
to see who can make theirs
last the longest.

What Lasts

I'm thinking of getting an artificial tree, she says.
It's September and I'm still picking up needles
from last year, she says. And they're so expensive,
the real ones, she says.

Well, you're at that age, her mother says—
kids, pets, practicalities—nothing wrong
with investing in something that lasts.
If you wish, you can have our old artificial one
lounging in the basement, the one we put up
before we downsized to the scrawny little thing
we toast these days with a snifter of brandy
on Christmas Eve, just the two of us,

sitting there in the quiet,
recalling the tree lot just outside the village,
the sweet smell of pine and spruce wafting from the piles,
your dad gripping one and tapping it hard
on the sidewalk to loosen the branches, the discussion
as to which one has the best shape, will hold its needles,
fits the room, rotating it this way and that
to hide the bare spot we will turn against the wall,
watching the high school kid tie it on the roof of the car,
the short drive to the tavern at the edge of the village square
for a spot of brandy while you and your brother
sip hot chocolate and play video games,

the stray needles in the corner of the room
the vacuum missed in January
reminding us in September
that before long we'll have the privilege
of living it all over again.

Secrets

As a child we had a four-party line.
Talk is cheap split four ways
reasoned post-Great Depression families
skeptical of the so-called post-war boom.
As a young Boomer, sometimes, when alone,

I would lift the receiver,
index finger on the black button
and release it slowly . . . carefully . . . cautiously
to avoid the telltale click followed by
the threatening, "If there's somebody on this line . . ."

The thick adult voices
spoke of today, yesterday, plans
and hopes for tomorrow—perhaps,
seems likely, don't really remember—
quotidian concerns

that felt like secrets then,
but history now,
filtered through the smudged lens
of their lives and my memory—
barely comprehensible.

Mother's Spaces

She stands before the living room window.
A neighborhood couple strolls down the street
hand in hand.

She touches the glass
as if to join them

(looks out
to see within?
looks within
to see out?)

then returns
to the dark rooms behind.

Dear Mother

I've written about you
but not of you. When
you lost your memory
60 years ago, you took mine
with you, left me with
the sepia moments: pressure
cooker meals on the table
4:30 sharp, Kool Aid
in the kitchen, telephone tucked
between ear and shoulder
as you ironed our lives
into tomorrow,
the car your escape
onto roads that always circled back—
a cage with no exit out. And later,
the dark years,
pious friends trumpeting
presumptuous prayers
to exorcise the demons
guarding treasures
I found buried at the bottom
of the old cedar chest:
fancy girls in fancy dresses
dancing to love songs
you played and prayed to the blank walls
of the cell where you fell asleep
and I finally awoke.
I am sorry. You did not know
how to say.
I am sorry. I did not know
how to listen.

On the Other Side of the Door

behind the knuckles rap
the room sings, filling the hallway
with Mario Lanza's tenorial boast—

Younger than springtime, am I,
gayer than laughter, am I.
I step inside.

Father takes a seat on the sofa
next to his new friend, Eleanor,
he introduces, but she does not look up.

Tears tickling a smile,
she stares at the phonograph
spinning joys and sorrows

like confetti in the wind.
He covers her hand with his,
the same gentle, yet insistent, touch

with which he cupped Mother's chin
through all those nursing home years—
Younger than springtime, are we,

he might have hummed as she curled
into dementia’s fetal fog.
Eleanor, he calls again, wishing

to rouse what refuses
to be recalled, while I,
youthful intruder, listen intently,

remember well Father’s kind touch,
Lanza’s mellifluous blessing,
so distant so near.

A Disagreement with My Dog

My dog loves someone I don't particularly like,
tugs me toward him during our morning walk,
like a kid toward a candy counter.
I could give you reasons why I don't like this man
but I sense you don't really care. And neither does my dog,
whose torso twists into a pretzel of joy
whenever she sees him. And furthermore,
if I started listing reasons, you might think—
no probably would think—*well, there's two sides*
to every story, and where would that leave me
but forced to list more reasons to support my case,
maybe make up a few that, who knows,
might be true, hell, come to think of it,
probably are true, despite her wriggling butt
and supplicated posture to receive this man's
cooed blessings and kindly fingers
to carry her through another sunny day
while I season and stir my righteous stew.

3 A.M.

Arms spread
open to the ready night

I climb hills of history,
the inevitable never enough

to soften the knowing—
and vice versa.

One dog's questioning look back
as he is led away. Another's

supine gaze of love and trust
as the vet inserts the needle.

One more, still young,
so perhaps our last,

curls against my thigh,
spreads open to receive

soft strokes to her tender belly
in our time, her gift

of reassurance
here and now.

Another 3 AM

It's another 3 AM and I'm lying in bed singing
the Star Spangled Banner silently to myself
when I forget to peer o'er the ramparts

and miss the rocket's red glare
(as Google mockingly points out),
causing me to wonder how I might fare

with My Country Tis of Thee or America the Beautiful
(not well as it turns out), and, tangentially related,
whether Miss Bruss, my grade school music teacher

with a huge round face and ruby red lips,
liked her job and died happy.
Moving on to the Pledge of Allegiance,

which, hand over heart hand on a Bible, I recite
as proudly and perfectly as my nine-year-old self
facing the flag in the corner

of Mrs. Borum's fourth grade classroom,
my dog yawns, stretches and pokes me in the side,
which, for no good reason, makes me wonder why God,

who so casually and regularly disappoints,
requires a bedside prayer when solace
can be found in fingers tangled in fur.

Worse Beginnings Beget Bad Endings

100 pages into Barbara Kingsolver's *Demon Copperhead*

Brutal.
From first chapter,
first page—oh, the awful things

people do to one another
described so eloquently
and graphically. I know,

you know, everyone knows
how the story ends, and it's bad.
We hear it every day—

ends ending badly.
But the beginnings even more brutal,
held close, wound tight around

hardened hearts, requiring short chapters
delivered mercifully in measured bursts
to allow one to catch one's breath, seek

shelter from the Dickensonian squalor
and cruelty we pretend is history,
though know, must know,

is now—our fictions
drawn onto pages
too true to be true.

Four Score

Nearly four score years ago
I entered the world,
a post WWII infant
presented as new breath
to a battered and exhausted generation
that saved the world.

Four score and five years earlier
Abraham Lincoln's message of deliverance
enjoined a war-weary generation
to rise again in civility
to honor their birth as a nation
four score and seven years ago.

Four score years from today
how shall our grandchildren
recognize that seed of deliverance
lying dormant beneath the turbulence
of our times and their days? How shall they
nurture it and carry it into posterity?

Blind Date—1969

Not quite blind
maybe out of focus
myopic ticket
to a bevy of bare shoulders
and pretty ankles
poking out of white sheets
college toga party
date. Walking back
to her dorm she swung
her Roman truncheon
like a cop on a beat
tapping car windows
for a ride
the black & white one
with a red bubble on top
obliging as I tried to explain
she wasn't thinking clearly
and we didn't need to go
to the place
he wished to take us
to no avail
so he pushes
and I push back
and there I am
on my back
ankle shackled
bunched and bundled
in my dirty white toga
staring into his
beet-red spittly face

my slowly in-focus date
lounging in a chair
chin in hand
bored as a juror
at an accountant's trial.
Cause and effect
go-figure karma
bad luck become
good luck I'm thinking
six months later
as the sergeant
at the induction station
who too wants
to take me to a place
I don't wish to go
tells me:
waivered
morally
temporarily
protocol
your record you see
need to determine
whether you're morally fit
to kill.

Secrets of the Universe

Standing along the periphery of the museum's cavernous room
a man stares at Jesus sharing a can of dog food
with a poor lady. Jesus looks like a hippie with a halo,
the poor lady so desperately rapt she'd eat the label on the can
if Jesus offered it to her.
If you can turn water into wine, he whispers to himself,
why not dog food into a porterhouse?
The man feels bold within the privacy of his thoughts.
Is language of the mind amoral, he wonders,
depending upon social context for measure and meaning?

In the center of the room sits a black lacquer bench
in front of a video monitor, on which the photographer
talks about his work. A woman in a black cashmere coat
sits at one end of the bench and a woman wearing red gloves
at the other end. The women look highbrow and snooty,
as if attending a museum exhibit were fodder
for that evening's cocktail conversation. Their cool beauty
makes the man feel vulnerable. Or maybe it's the naked men
in the photographs. Perhaps he was prematurely critical
of Jesus and is in need of a measure of mercy himself.

The man squats behind the bench in front of the monitor,
loses his balance, and touches the bench to steady himself.
Both women glance over their shoulder, then turn away.
The woman on his left crosses her right leg over the left;
the woman on his right tugs her skirt over her knee.

The photographer, an impish, kind-looking man, speaks
solemnly and reverently about his work, like a priest
dispensing the secrets of the universe.

The man thinks about how after he leaves the museum
he promised his wife he'd do the grocery shopping
and the lines will be long, but tomorrow's Monday
and next week is going to be busy—

One must look closely.

The photographer's words jerk him back into the room,
the black lacquer bench, the video monitor, two women,
one on each side like children on a teeter-totter,
he the fulcrum, his eye a shutter recording the events
of this room, this life, simple statements of being and yearning
    and—

the woman wearing red gloves turns, as if she senses someone
watching. The man looks quickly away, suddenly aware
that he has been staring without seeing. Not looking

makes him wish to see her anew, to notice her existence,
to fix her red hands indelibly in his mind. The woman
at the other end of the bench recrosses her legs,
slips her heel out of her shoe and dangles it like bait
from the toes of her slender foot. On cue, both women turn.
Philanderer? Voyeur?
Is that what they think?

Did this woman buy fire engine red gloves
to highlight or hide the beauty of her hands?
Is this other woman unaware of the loveliness of her ankle?
No, they present themselves as argument
to which he feels compelled to respond.

The man no longer cares whether he disturbs these women.
He's tried to remain inconspicuous but they insist
on being distracted. If he were a double amputee
sitting on a street corner, they would not look
but he bets they can't resist,
say, a cough or his tapping his fingers lightly on the bench.
He does both and both women glance back disapprovingly.

Being right makes the man feel sad,
as if he has powers he doesn't deserve.
But these powers are trite and meaningless,
completely appropriate for a man
visiting a museum for whom sadness suddenly
feels warm and worth preserving.

The man stares at the monitor, imagining himself an artist
for whom sadness is an opportunity to capture beauty.

From the corner of his eye, he senses movement; he turns
as the woman with the red gloves steps through the door
and disappears. He catches his breath, scanning the room
for the woman in the black coat who, too, has disappeared.

The man touches the bench to steady himself.

Christmas Eve Service

From the back of the cathedral
a young man holding a crucifix high
leads two young guitarists
slowly down the nave
toward the altar singing

Eat his body, drink his blood,
then we can begin to talk of love.

My children look up
as if hoping I might explain
these strange pagan lyrics.
I glance uneasily at my wife
as the cross settles at the altar,

then stare ahead as ushers
release alternate rows of worshipers
from their pews. Heads bowed,
fingers clasped solemnly across their chest
they shuffle slowly toward the altar

and priest holding the sacramental body and blood
to open-mouth supplicants
waiting like newly hatched fledglings
their spiritual nourishment.

When the usher arrives at my pew,
I hesitate. My wife waits patiently
for me to step forward into the aisle.

I step back to let her and others pass.
The possibility of a little more love in my life
notwithstanding, I've lost my appetite.

Choice

The weatherman tracks an off-shore front
over there, not here, where skies remain fair,
until we flip the channel or click the page

and are confronted with forecasts filled with rage,
Adam's ill-advised bite
condensed into today's discouraging bytes.

Do not gaze heavenward
and dream the miraculous return
to the mythos of Eden and halcyon days.

Do not, like Adam, ignore what Eve understood:
what's near is here—the apple our choice
to give love a voice.

Yes Love

If I were but a word in an unremarkable sentence,
which I surely am,
what kind of word might that be?
A multisyllabic word whose meaning
I would have to look up?

A proud and proper noun,
betrothed to a flag-waving adjective
upon whose generosity my identity depends?
A knee-jiggling verb itching for action
yesterday or today?

Perhaps a pushy preposition modifying
some random object with or without its permission?
Or maybe a conjunctive word, such as *but,*
upon which, as Steven Dunn aptly notes,
so much depends? Yes,

but, that word,
no, these words—
yes   *but*
the sibilant urgency of *yes* tempered
by the cautious hesitancy of *but,*

which, while some might interpret as a precursor
to argument, I view as an invitation
to connection—the conjoining of my words
with your words in search of company, community,

consensus and, yes,
love? Yes, *love,*
that word—but
wait, no,
these words—
Yes   *Love.*

On Leaving Pamplona—1973

for Linda

in the early morning hours
standing at the edge of the plaza
gazing into the detritus
of celebration now asleep
I emptied my pockets
into the empty square
pocket change too heavy
to carry into this new life
imagined
eventually found

four years later

when you appeared
and together
we attached ourselves
to the axis
of a small bed
next to a large window
watching the sun rise
over Maumee Bay
and beyond
into a new life
imagined
and finally found

Mashed Potatoes Love

For you
I beat the potatoes
mercilessly,
mash and whip their soft bodies
into lumpless white peaks
holding the volcanic crater
into which you drop
a slice of pepper-flaked butter
that pools then flows like lava
down that smooth white mountain
and onto your waiting fork.

Mating

On the deck rail
two northern flickers
bob and weave
like a couple of French men
trying to decide
which cheek to kiss.

Skittish and shy
gestures of love and desire
we anthropomorphize.
Will she arch her back,
move tail to the side
to receive the cloacal kiss,

we ask, like announcers
introducing a Telemundo soap opera.
She pauses, spreads her wings
and flies away. He pauses,
spreads his wings,
then follows.

You stand and head inside.
I pause, then follow.

Good Grief

Grief, so common, so personal—
the weight of a breath,
the silence of a sigh
known and owned.

I have no untimely deaths to grieve
(Are there timely deaths? Yes,
I think we might all agree while remaining
politely hesitant to name names),

but I do know the grief of forgetting
what was once loved,
the grief of remembering
what was once loved.

But *good grief*—how shall I situate it?
As an oxymoronic response
to a world that willfully refuses
to acknowledge what it knows to be true?

Or as a blessing bestowed? Yes, I am blessed
to one day have much to grieve because
I have had much to love. And, yes, it is good
to celebrate today what I will one day grieve.

Rest Now

say goodnight
to this aspirin-addled world
sink softly
into the luxury of slumber
set the saw upon
the stack of lumber
from which tomorrow’s tasks
arise

I Honor

this river of words
its streams and tributaries
rapids and eddies

the slow melt of mystery
and memory
rippling through

this river of words
seeking all ways
to gentler waters

About the Author

Robert Nordstrom was raised in Ohio, where as a child he climbed trees in suburbia searching for a way up and out. After a stint in Vietnam, a number of years sweating in front of restaurant kitchen broilers, a year in Paris with his wife Linda, he finally found his way to Wisconsin where he obtained an MA in creative writing from the University of Wisconsin-Milwaukee. In 2018, he and his wife moved to Oregon to be closer to children and grandchildren.

For more than 30 years he worked as an editor and writer for various trade and scholarly publications and taught writing at the university level. After retiring he drove a school bus for several years teaching high schoolers how to respond when an adult says good morning and informing kindergarteners that it's probably best they not lick the seat in front of them.

Nordstrom's poetry, essays, and fiction appear in numerous national and regional literary publications. His poem "Old Lovers" won the 2014 Hal Prize, and his 2015 collection *The Sacred Monotony of Breath* garnered honorable mention from the Council for Wisconsin Writers. His collection *Dust on the Sill* (Kelsay Books) was published in 2023.

www.ingramcontent.com/pod-product-compliance
Lightning Source LLC
LaVergne TN
LVHW090617110826
845146LV00001B/422

9798901468340